Contents

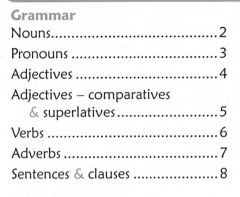

Nouns

WHAT ARE NOUNS?

Nouns are the names of people, animals, places and things. These are all nouns:

girl, book, shoe, river, tree, rat, boat

Not all nouns are things you can touch. They can be ideas or concepts. These are nouns too:

history, music, truth, hunger, love

COMMON & PROPER NOUNS

Common nouns

Common nouns are the general names of things. These are all common nouns:

boy, mushroom, leg, television, zebra, paint

Proper nouns

A proper noun is the name of a particular person, place or thing. A proper noun always begins with a capital letter. These are all proper nouns:

Alice, Wednesday, India, Lincoln, November, Tesco

COLLECTIVE NOUNS

Names for groups of things are called collective nouns. Here are some examples:

A crowd of people   A team of footballers

A class of pupils   A litter of puppies

A flock of sheep   A nest of vipers

A herd of cows   A pack of submarines

QUICK QUIZ

1 Pick out the nouns in these sentences:
   a A crowd gathered at the stadium in Manchester.
   b Judy had a dream about a horse.
2 Which of the nouns in question 1 are proper nouns?

Pronouns

A pronoun is a word used in place of a noun. Pronouns help you avoid writing the same noun over and over again. Look at this example:

Emily lent Emily's skateboard to Emily's dad.

It sounds better if you use the pronoun 'her' rather than repeating Emily's name all the time:

Emily lent her skateboard to her dad.

Here are some other pronouns you could use in your writing:

> **Pronouns**
> I, me, you, he, she, it, him, her, we, us, they, them, my, mine, your, yours, his, hers, its, our, ours, your, yours, their, theirs

Kirk has a new guitar. Kirk bought the guitar on Friday. Kirk has a new guitar. He bought it on Friday.

The aliens are very clever. The aliens have two brains. The aliens are very clever. They have two brains.

MAKE SURE THE MEANING IS CLEAR

When you use pronouns, make sure it's clear who is doing what. In this example, it's not clear who the people are, or what's been poisoned.

He was sure she was trying to kill him. When she bought him it, he wondered if it was poisoned.

This version is better. It's clear who and what the pronouns stand for.

Harry was sure Jess was trying to kill him. When she bought him an ice cream, he wondered if it was poisoned.

 Always read through your writing to check it's clear who or what the pronouns stand for.

QUICK QUIZ

Make this sound better by replacing some of the nouns with pronouns:
Emma has a pet crocodile. Emma's brother is scared of the crocodile so Emma's brother won't go in Emma's bedroom.

Adjectives

Adjectives are describing words. They give more information about nouns. Use adjectives to make your descriptions more interesting or accurate.

The grumpy farmer is pointing at this brilliant example.

'grumpy' is the adjective that describes 'farmer'.

'brilliant' is the adjective that describes 'example'.

CHOOSING ADJECTIVES

Choose the most interesting and descriptive adjectives you can think of. Avoid everyday adjectives like 'good' and 'nice'.

a nice orange ✗

a sweet, juicy orange ✔

 Look up dull adjectives in a thesaurus to find more interesting alternatives.

Adjectives with similar meanings can create different effects.

an old car   a vintage car

Avoid using adjectives that don't add anything to the noun, as in 'dreadful disaster'. Disasters are always dreadful.

DON'T USE TOO MANY ADJECTIVES AT ONCE

Don't use long lists of adjectives as they sound awkward. Decide which are the most important features.

the tiny, hot, green, exotic, deserted island ✗

the tiny, deserted island ✔

Listing two or three adjectives is fine, but don't do it too often, or your writing will become difficult to read.

QUICK QUIZ

1 Pick out the adjectives in these sentences:
   a The tall girl wore a stripy jumper.   **b** It was a cold, wet morning.
2 Improve these sentences by adding adjectives:
   a The captain remained on the ship.
   b The children crept up the stairs.

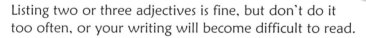

Adjectives – comparatives & superlatives

COMPARATIVES

Adjectives can be used to compare one thing with another.
For most short adjectives, just add 'er' to the end of the adjective.

Tariq is older than Damian.   My phone is louder than yours.

For longer adjectives, use 'more' or 'less' with the adjective.

Caesar was more powerful than Brutus.

Silver is less valuable than gold.

 Never use 'more' and 'er' together.
You are more quicker than me. ✗

SUPERLATIVES

Adjectives can also be used to say which of a group of things is the best, worst and so on. For most short adjectives, just add 'est' to the adjective.

Tariq is the oldest in his class.   My phone is the loudest you can buy.

For longer adjectives, use 'most' or 'least' with the adjective.

Cleopatra was the most beautiful woman in Egypt.

This is the least comfortable sofa I own.

 Never use 'most' and 'est' together.
You are the most quickest runner. ✗

Some adjectives don't follow the rules. Make sure you know these:

Adjective	Comparative	Superlative
good	better	best
bad	worse	worst
little	less	least
many	more	most

QUICK QUIZ

James, Kyle and Liam are brothers. James is 12, Kyle is 14 and Liam is 17.
Complete these sentences with a comparative or superlative:

1 Kyle is _____ than Liam.   **2** Kyle is _____ than James.
3 James is the _____ brother.

Verbs

In general, a verb is a 'doing' word, like 'run', 'sing', 'walk', 'dance', ...
Verbs can also be 'being' words, like 'am', 'are', 'is', 'were', ...

The dog sniffed the ground.

Sherlock looked up.

The boat is speeding.

Hannah is a keen gardener.

Sometimes the verb is two words.
(This is called a verb chain.)

Don't forget Most verbs have one form when used with 'I', 'we', 'you' or 'they', but a different form with 'he', 'she' or 'it'.
I bake cakes.   He bakes cakes.

PRESENT, PAST & FUTURE

The tense of a verb tells you whether the action happens right now, in the past or in the future.

Present tense (the action is happening now)
Eric kicks the ball.   or   Eric is kicking the ball.

Past tense (the action has already happened)
Eric kicked the ball.   or   Eric was kicking the ball.

Future tense (the action has yet to happen)
Eric is going to kick the ball.   or   Eric will kick the ball.

 You can't always add 'ed' to the verb to get the past tense.
I eated a sandwich. ✗   She writed a letter. ✗
I ate a sandwich. ✔   She wrote a letter. ✔

QUICK QUIZ

1 Pick out the verbs in these sentences:
   a Madison scored a goal.   **b** Lucas cycles to school.
2 Re-write these sentences in the past tense:
   a They own a farm.   **b** I am feeling cold.

Adverbs

Adverbs give more detail about what is happening. For example, an adverb might tell you how, when or where something happened. Look at this sentence:

He played his trumpet.

It doesn't tell you how, when or where he played his trumpet. You can use adverbs like 'loudly', 'yesterday' or 'upstairs' to give this extra detail.

He played his trumpet loudly. ◄──── (This is how the trumpet was played.)

He played his trumpet yesterday. ◄──── (This is when the trumpet was played.)

He played his trumpet upstairs. ◄──── (This is where the trumpet was played.)

Here are some more examples of adverbs:

Adverbs for 'how'	Adverbs for 'when'	Adverbs for 'where'
carefully, easily, fast, happily, heavily, noisily, quickly, softly, well	earlier, later, never, now, often, sometimes, then, today, tomorrow	away, downstairs, everywhere, here, indoors, nowhere, outside, there

When a group of words acts like an adverb, it is called an adverbial.

She threw the boomerang in the garden.

Adverbs can go at the start, middle or end of a sentence.

Slowly, the girl opened the gate.

The girl slowly opened the gate.

The girl opened the gate slowly.

Tip When you're writing, try putting the adverb in different positions to see which sounds best.

⚠ Sometimes it's better to use a more powerful verb rather than an adverb and a verb.

He talked quietly to the elf. ➤ He whispered to the elf.

Which word is an adverb?

1 small, badger, sweetly, it   **2** quick, quicker, quickly, quickest

Sentences & clauses

SIMPLE SENTENCES

A sentence is made up of clauses. Each clause contains one verb.
A sentence with only one clause (one verb) is called a simple sentence.

Colin rode his scooter.

There is only one verb, so this is a simple sentence.

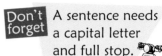

Don't forget A sentence needs a capital letter and full stop.

Any sentence with only one verb is a simple sentence, even if the sentence is quite long, like this one:

In the middle of the night, Colin rode his scooter along the pavement.

The following sentence has two verbs, so it has two clauses. This means it is not a simple sentence.

Colin stopped at the traffic lights when they turned red.

This is a clause.   This is another clause.

COMPOUND SENTENCES

Two simple sentences joined together with 'and', 'but' or 'or' make a compound sentence.
Use 'and' when you want to link similar things.

The windows rattled. The floorboards creaked.

The windows rattled and the floorboards creaked.

You don't always need to repeat the person's name if the same person is the subject of both clauses.

Alice ate popcorn and Alice drank lemonade.

Alice ate popcorn and drank lemonade.

Use 'but' when you want to show differences or opposites.

I liked Paris. I didn't like Venice.

I liked Paris but I didn't like Venice.

Don't link loads of sentences together with 'and' or 'and then' or your writing will sound boring.

I went shopping and bought a coat and then visited my aunt and had lunch and then got the bus home and went to bed.

Sentences & clauses

COMPLEX SENTENCES

A complex sentence has one main clause that makes sense on its own. It also has one or more subordinate clauses that give extra information about the main clause. Subordinate clauses don't really make sense without the main clause.

Alan wore a wet suit because the sea was cold.

This is the main clause.

This is the subordinate clause. It gives extra information about the main clause.

Your writing will sound jerky if you use only simple sentences. Complex sentences will make your writing flow better. Use words like these to link clauses together:

> **Linking words (conjunctions)**
> after, although, as, because, before, despite, if, since, so, unless, until, when, where, while

Varying the position of subordinate clauses will make your writing more interesting. In this example the subordinate clause comes first:

Unless help arrived, Alan was in trouble.

When the subordinate clause goes first, you need a comma after it.

You can also embed extra information in the middle of a sentence, like this:

Alan, who was late already, struggled to move.

The commas show the start and end of the subordinate clause.

QUICK QUIZ

Choose one of these words to complete each sentence.

1 James is only five _____ he can play chess.
2 I can't buy it _____ I get my pocket money.
3 _____ Bethany went home, I went to bed.

so
after
but
until
if

Sentence punctuation

CAPITAL LETTERS & FULL STOPS

A sentence should start with a capital letter and end with a full stop (or a question mark or exclamation mark if needed).

Without capital letters and full stops it's difficult to know where one sentence ends and the next begins.

Start each sentence with a capital letter.

Bert had been flying all day. He was beginning to run out of fuel.

End each sentence with a full stop.

QUESTION MARKS

A sentence that asks a question needs a question mark instead of a full stop.

Is that the last biscuit?

EXCLAMATION MARKS

You need an exclamation mark instead of a full stop if you want to show strong feelings or urgency.

You can use them for commands

Run!

or to show someone is shouting

I hate you!

or to show surprise.

I didn't know you were a doctor!

COMMAS

Commas help make the meaning of a sentence clear.

Ali saw a pig, and a man playing golf.

Without the comma you might think the pig was playing golf!

You can also use commas to write a list.

He played for Fulham, West Ham United, Southampton and Arsenal.

Commas are also used to surround extra information added to sentences.

Sonia, who works at the garden centre, grew this year's biggest turnip.

QUICK QUIZ

Put in the missing sentence punctuation:

the noise started suddenly what a racket where was it coming from Kate checked the kitchen the bathroom the lounge and under her bed

Speech marks

You should only use <u>speech marks</u> when someone is actually speaking.
Put the speech marks around the <u>actual words</u> that are <u>spoken</u>.

You can use double or single speech marks (" " or ' ').

Say who is speaking.

"Your new carpet looks fast," said Lenny.

Use a capital letter when someone starts speaking.

Put a comma before the closing speech mark if the sentence carries on.

Don't forget Start a <u>new paragraph</u> when a different person speaks.

You can say who is speaking before they speak.

You still need to start the speech with a capital letter.

Christina screeched to a halt and said, "It goes like a rocket."

You need to put a comma before the opening speech mark.

End the sentence with a full stop before the closing speech mark.

If the words that are spoken are a question, make sure you use
a <u>question mark</u>. "Can I have a go on it?" asked Lenny.

You can also use <u>exclamation marks</u> in speech.

Christina shouted, "No way, you crashed the last one!"

REPORTED SPEECH

Only use speech marks for actual speech, <u>not</u> when you are reporting
what someone said.

Lenny asked if he could have a go on the flying carpet.

Lenny's exact words are not used, so <u>don't</u> use speech marks.

 If you're reading a story at the moment, have a look at how the
author handles speech.

QUICK QUIZ

Add speech marks where necessary to these sentences:
1 I'll do it later, said Yola.   2 Jen asked, Why now?
3 Megan said she hated washing up.   4 Attack! cried the centurion.

Paragraphs

Using paragraphs will make your writing easier to read. A paragraph can be long or short, but all the sentences within it must be related. You need to start a new paragraph when something changes.

WHEN SOMETHING NEW HAPPENS

Each time something new happens, start a new paragraph.

The car jumping onto the pavement is a new event, so you need a new paragraph.

Start the new paragraph on a new line, with the first word indented. ('Indent' means leave a gap.)

Superpup wondered where all the traffic had come from. Crossing the road had never been a problem before.

Suddenly, a car jumped onto the pavement. It was heading straight for Superpup.

JUMPING TO A DIFFERENT TIME

If you jump to a different time, start a new paragraph. You could start the new paragraph with one of these words or phrases:

after, after a while, before, before this, earlier, eventually, last year, later, the next day, tomorrow, yesterday

Paragraphs make it easier to read.

There is a jump in time, so start a new paragraph.

On the first morning, we all had to go on deck. There, the admiral of the fleet gave us a talk on the importance of writing in paragraphs.

Later that afternoon, the wind picked up and the ship began to roll from side to side. I began to feel sea sick, which was made worse by ...

MOVING TO A DIFFERENT PLACE

Start a new paragraph when you start writing about a different place.

This paragraph is set on the planet.

The setting now changes to the spaceship, so you need a new paragraph.

James ran as fast as he could to escape the strange creatures. He was beginning to tire, but there was nowhere to hide on the barren planet.

Back on board the spaceship, Elizabeth was playing astro tennis. Her robot opponent, Dax, was about to ...

Paragraphs

WRITING ABOUT A DIFFERENT PERSON

Start a new paragraph when you introduce a new character, or move from one character to another.

David was looking forward to his birthday. He was having a big party with a DJ. All his friends were coming, even Jenny.

This paragraph is about David (and his party).

Jenny used to go to David's school, but she moved to London last summer. She was always ...

This bit is about Jenny, so start a new paragraph.

WHEN A DIFFERENT PERSON SPEAKS

When you are writing a story, start a new paragraph each time the speaker changes.

The speaker has changed, so start a new paragraph.

"Where were you on Thursday afternoon?" asked Inspector Partridge.
"Are you accusing me of murder?" replied his wife, outraged.
"Everyone's a suspect," said the inspector, "even you, darling."

It's still the inspector speaking here, so you don't need a new paragraph.

Don't forget

Put speech marks around the actual words that are spoken (see page 11).

CHANGING SUBJECT

In factual writing, you should start a new paragraph when you change subject or bring in a new idea. Look at this extract from a letter:

I have just received the red tape I ordered. Despite being promised next day delivery, it has taken three weeks to arrive.

The first paragraph is about the slow delivery.

Furthermore, I am unhappy with the tape itself. It is far too sticky and impossible to use without getting tangled up in it.

The stickiness is a different subject, so it needs its own paragraph.

Some people leave a line space between paragraphs rather than indenting the first line. It's up to you which method you use, but don't mix them.

Apostrophes

I'm is an informal way of writing I am. The apostrophe shows where letters have been missed out. Here are some examples you should know:

I am ➔ I'm	I will ➔ I'll
you are ➔ you're	she will ➔ she'll
she is ➔ she's	who is ➔ who's
it is ➔ it's	does not ➔ doesn't
we are ➔ we're	did not ➔ didn't
they are ➔ they're	is not ➔ isn't
I have ➔ I've	cannot ➔ can't
you have ➔ you've	should not ➔ shouldn't
I had ➔ I'd	do not ➔ don't
I would ➔ I'd	will not ➔ won't

The 'o' from 'not' is missing, so the apostrophe goes here.

Don't use contractions in formal writing, such as reports or formal letters.

This one's different. It's won't not willn't.

POSSESSIVE APOSTROPHES

Apostrophes can also be used to show that something belongs to somebody. Just add an apostrophe followed by an 's'.

the tail that belongs to the lion ➔ the lion's tail

the coats that belong to the men ➔ the men's coats

Words ending in 's'

If the word already ends in 's' you can add an apostrophe with or without an extra 's'.

the lion that belongs to James ➔ James's lion ✔ or James' lion ✔

But if the word that ends in 's' is a group of people, you must not add the extra 's'.

the hats that belong to the girls ➔ the girls' hats ✔ not the girls's hats ✘

Never use an apostrophe in pronouns like its, hers, yours or theirs.
The dog hates it's kennel. ✘   The dog hates its kennel. ✔

QUICK QUIZ

Fill in the missing apostrophes:

1 a Tina cant swim.   **b** Its a boy!   **c** Shell be here later.
2 a Marks watch had stopped.   **b** The ladies bags were lost.

Spelling by breaking up words

SYLLABLES

Breaking a word up into syllables will help you spell it a bit at a time.

li - on

Span - ish

'Conductor' has three syllables.

con - duc - tor

'Dancer' has two syllables.

glad - i - a - tor

dan - cer

You have to be careful with some words as they are not pronounced the way they are spelt. You can learn how to spell these words by saying them in your head the way they are written.

Wed - nes - day

You don't normally pronounce this 'd'.

You usually say 'Wens - day'.

ve - ge - ta - ble

Saying it this way will help you spell it.

Feb - ru - ar - y

You don't usually hear this 'r'.

COMPOUND WORDS

A compound word is a long word that is made by joining shorter words together. Breaking a compound word into shorter words will help you spell it.

birthday = birth + day

classmate = class + mate

spaceship = space + ship

QUICK QUIZ

1   How many syllables do these words have?
    a tadpole   **b** difficult   **c** introduction   **d** umbrella
2   Use these six words to make three compound words.

case   ball
flakes   corn
        eye   book

Spelling rules

'q' is followed by 'u', then another vowel

In English words, 'q' is always followed by 'u' and then another vowel.

equipment queen boutique

quality

liquid equator quiet

No words end in 'v'

English words never end in 'v'. If a word sounds like it ends in 'v', it must end 've'.

 detective

solve

secretive

serve

active

> There are very few exceptions to this rule. The exceptions are abbreviations like 'lav' or slang words like 'spiv'.

No words end in 'j'

English words never end in 'j'. Words that sound like they end in 'j' usually end 'ge' or 'dge'.

 bridge

 judge

luggage

wedge

'i' before 'e', except after 'c'

shield

This rule's pretty good if the 'ie' or 'ei' makes a long 'ee' sound.

'i' before 'e'	except after 'c'
grief, piece, shield, thief	ceiling, deceive, receipt, receive

The rule doesn't work for these words because they don't have a long 'ee' sound: eight, foreign, height, leisure, neighbour, science, their, weight

⚠ There are a few words that do have a long 'ee' sound but don't follow the rule: caffeine, protein, seize, weir, weird, Neil, Sheila

QUICK QUIZ

Choose the correct spelling.   **a** qwick, quick, qiuck
b curve, curv, kurve   **c** badje, badj, badge   **d** believ, beleive, believe

Homophones

Homophones are words that sound the same, but have different spellings and meanings. A common mistake is to use the wrong version.

The ball went through the racket.

She threw the ball.

a pair of socks

a pear

Here are some other homophones you need to take care with:

She **ate** an apple.	Spiders have **eight** legs.
I've **been** to the zoo.	Would you like a jelly **bean**?
I couldn't **find** my pen.	He was **fined** £50.
She has curly **hair**.	A **hare** is like a rabbit.
Come **here** now!	Did you **hear** that noise?
We have a **new** dog.	I **knew** his brother.
It's a **piece** of cake!	I need some **peace** and quiet.
Turn **right**, not left.	I am going to **write** a letter.
The shop has a half-price **sale**.	The wind caught the boat's **sail**.
I **saw** that film at the cinema.	I've got **sore** feet from walking.
You **see** with your eyes.	Fish swim in the **sea**.
Where do you live?	You **wear** clothes.
Which of these do you want?	The **witch** cast a spell.
Two halves make a **whole**.	Rover dug a **hole** in the garden.
Wood comes from trees.	What **would** you like?

here and **there**	it's **their** house	**they're** coming
one plus one is **two**	he's going **to** a party	it's **too** late
rich and **poor**	**pour** a drink	a dog's **paw**	**pore** in your skin

Correct the spelling mistakes in these sentences.

a "I'm board," yawned Jack. **b** I walked on the beach with bear feet.
c Ben jumped hire than Sam. **d** You need flower to make a cake.

Plurals

FOR MOST PLURALS JUST ADD 'S'

When you have more than one thing, it's called a plural.
For most nouns, you just add 's' to get the plural.

one drink → two drinks   one bag → five bags

one toe → ten toes   an apple → some apples

Sometimes you need to add 'es'
If the word ends in a hissing sound, you need to add 'es'.

glass → glasses   box → boxes   dish → dishes

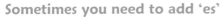

If you just added 's', you wouldn't really hear it.
Try saying 'glasss', 'boxs', 'dishs' or 'witchs'.

witch → witches

Never use apostrophes for plurals. This mistake is often found on shop signs. See if you can spot any next time you're out shopping.
Cauliflower's half price. ✗   Two meal's for the price of one. ✗
Cauliflowers half price. ✔   Two meals for the price of one. ✔

WORDS ENDING IN 'F' OR 'FE'

For most words ending in 'f' or 'fe', you change the ending
to 'ves' to make the plural.

wife → wives   hoof → hooves   thief → thieves

However, for some words you do just add an 's'.

roof → roofs   chef → chefs   gulf → gulfs

WORDS ENDING IN 'O'

There are no easy rules for words ending in 'o'.
For many words ending in 'o', you make the plural by adding 'es'.

potato → potatoes   tomato → tomatoes   hero → heroes

For other words ending in 'o', you make the plural by adding 's'.

piano → pianos   radio → radios   photo → photos

Some words ending in
'o' can be made plural by   tornado → tornadoes or tornados
adding either 'es' or 's'.
                                   flamingo → flamingoes or flamingos

Plurals

For some words ending in 'y', you make the plural by adding 's'. For others you need to change the 'y' to 'ies'. Follow these rules:

If the letter before the 'y' is a vowel (a, e, i, o, u), add 's'

monkey → monkeys   day → days   toy → toys

The letter before the 'y' is a vowel ...   ... so add an 's'.

If the letter before the 'y' is a consonant, the 'y' becomes 'ies'

cherry → cherries   copy → copies   ice lolly → ice lollies

The letter before the 'y' is a consonant ...   ... so 'y' becomes 'ies'.

PLURALS THAT BREAK THE RULES

Some words have strange plurals, so you just have to learn them.

foot → feet   man → men   child → children

tooth → teeth   ox → oxen   mouse → mice

For some animals and fish, you use the same word for the plural.

one deer → two deer   one moose → two moose

one sheep → two sheep   one cod → two cod

These nouns do not have a plural at all.

aluminium   geography   flour

These nouns are only used as plurals.

cattle   trousers   scissors

You need to say 'a pair of scissors' if you only have one. You can't say 'a scissor' or 'a scissors'.

QUICK QUIZ

What are the plurals of these words?

a hat   **b** fox   **c** beach   **d** leaf

e disco   **f** donkey   **g** berry   **h** woman

Prefixes & suffixes

Recognising how words are built up will help you spell them.

PREFIXES

A prefix is added to the beginning of a word to change its meaning.

un + tidy = untidy

| The prefix 'un' means 'not'. | So this means not tidy. |

mis + behave = misbehave

| The prefix 'mis' means 'badly'. | So this means behave badly. |

Here are some other common prefixes:

Prefix	Meaning	Examples
il-	not	illegal, illogical
pre-	before	preheat, premature
re-	again	reapply, reconnect
sub-	under	submarine, substandard

Prefix

SUFFIXES

A suffix is added to the end of a word to change its meaning.

duck + ling = duckling

| The suffix 'ling' means 'a little one'. | So this means a little duck. |

Japan + ese = Japanese

| The suffix 'ese' means 'belonging to'. |

Here are some other common suffixes:

Suffix	Meaning or use	Examples
-able	can do	drinkable, washable
-ance	changes a verb into a noun	disturbance, performance
-ful	full of	colourful, truthful
-less	lack of	fearless, worthless

 Sometimes the spelling of the root word changes when you add a suffix. For example: beauty + ful = beautyful ✗ beautiful ✔

QUICK QUIZ

Use these prefixes, root words and suffixes to make three new words.
mal-, un-, function, child, break, -ish, -able

Reading fiction & non-fiction

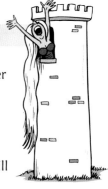

READING FICTION

Fiction is writing that is made up. For example, *Tom's Midnight Garden* by Philippa Pearce and the Harry Potter series by J.K. Rowling are fictional stories as they have been made up by their authors.

Stories come in many different genres (types), such as adventure, fairy tales, fantasy, horror, science fiction and westerns. Reading lots of stories from different genres will help you come up with ideas for your own stories.

 When you're reading a story, try to guess what will happen next. Were your predictions correct or did the author surprise you?

READING NON-FICTION

Non-fiction is factual writing. Newspaper reports, leaflets and history books are all examples of non-fiction.

A non-fiction book often has an index to help you find the information you're looking for. Look down the alphabetical list for the word you're interested in, and it will tell you which pages to go to.

FACT & OPINION

Although non-fiction is factual writing, the author often includes his or her own opinions on the subject. You need to be able to tell the difference between fact and opinion.

Rugby Union was last played at the Olympic Games in 1924. It's a great shame that it's no longer an Olympic event.

This is a fact.

This is the author's opinion.

Different writers should agree on the facts (unless one of them has made a mistake!) but they may have different opinions. For example, writers should agree what happened but they may disagree why it happened.

Tip You should read several books on a topic to get a balanced view.

QUICK QUIZ

Are these books fiction or non-fiction?

1 Encyclopedia   **2** Jack and the Beanstalk   **3** How to Play the Flute

Seven top tips for reading tests

1. READ EVERYTHING

In your reading test you'll be given two booklets: a reading booklet and an answer booklet with the questions in.

At the start of your reading test you'll be given some time to read the reading booklet. Make sure you read everything, and I mean everything – even headings and labels may help you answer a question.

2. GET YOUR ANSWER FROM THE RIGHT PLACE

At the start of each section in the answer booklet, there are instructions telling you where to look for the answers. Make sure you only look at these pages in the reading booklet when answering.

Check that you're looking at the correct pages in the reading booklet.

SECTION 1

These questions are about *The New World* (pages 4 and 5).

3. READ THE QUESTION CAREFULLY

Read each question carefully. If necessary, read it again to make sure you understand what you are being asked to do.

Follow the instructions. Don't just tick one box.

According to the leaflet on page 39, which of these facilities are available at Hinkton Library? Tick **three**.

internet access	✓	drinks machine	
writing workshops		photocopier	✓
audio books	✓	Sunday opening	

4. DON'T WASTE TIME ON QUESTIONS YOU CAN'T DO

Don't worry if you can't do some of the questions, just leave them out. There will be lots of questions you can do, so concentrate on those. You can always come back to any you missed out at the end.

Seven top tips for reading tests

5. GET YOUR ANSWER FROM THE READING BOOKLET

Always try to find the answer in the reading booklet. Don't just write the first answer that pops into your head. Even if you think you remember what the reading booklet said, you should go back and read that bit again to make sure you're right.

What was it like in the woods in the play on page 33? Ring **one** of these words.

| wet | dark | cold | warm |

Don't just guess what it was like in the woods. You need to read the play to find out.

If you *really* can't find the answer to a multiple choice question, then you might as well have a guess – marks are not taken off for wrong answers.

6. SCAN FOR KEY WORDS

When trying to find the answer in a long passage of text you should scan for a key word from the question.

When was the Louvre Museum first opened to the public?

Scanning the passage below for the key word 'opened' will help you find the answer. Or you could try to spot a number that looks like a year.

The Louvre Museum is located in Paris, the capital of France. It is one of the world's most visited art museums. The Louvre was first opened to the public as a museum in 1793, during the French Revolution. There are 35 000 works of art on display at the museum, including the famous *Mona Lisa* painting by Leonardo de Vinci.

Once you've found what you were scanning for, read that part of the text carefully to make sure it gives the answer you were after.

The Louvre Museum first opened to the public in 1793.

7. IF YOU FINISH EARLY ...

If you finish early, don't just put your pen down and wait for everyone else to finish – now's the time to try any questions you missed out. If you still have time left, check the rest of your answers.

Types of poetry

Poems create different moods and feelings. Many poems give a message, or make you think about an idea. They don't have to rhyme, but many do. Here are some different types of poem you might come across:

LIMERICKS

A limerick is a humorous poem with five lines. Lines 1, 2 and 5 rhyme, and lines 3 and 4 rhyme. All limericks follow the same rhythm.

> There once was a fellow named Jay,
> Who rode a fine steed that was grey;
> Thrown over a hedge,
> He made it his pledge,
> To find a new horse straight away.

HAIKU

A haiku is a three-line poem that doesn't rhyme. There are five syllables in the first line, seven in the second, and five in the last.

Going yesterday,
Today, tonight ... the wild geese
Have all gone, honking. (Taniguchi Buson)

Originally from Japan, haiku are traditionally about the seasons.

SHAPE POEMS

A shape poem uses the layout of the words to show what the poem is about. Shape poems are sometimes called concrete poems.

On rolling hills of Spain, you're really such a pain, with each new trough and old peak, you make my legs quite weak.

CLERIHEWS

A clerihew is a humorous poem. It has four lines, which rhyme in pairs. It is usually about a person, who is named in the first line.

Sir Humphry Davy
Abominated gravy.
He lived in the odium
Of having discovered sodium.

Did you know? Clerihews are named after Edmund Clerihew Bentley. He wrote this one at school when he was bored in a science lesson.

Imagery in poetry

Poems often have really imaginative descriptions which help create a picture in your mind.

SIMILES

A simile is a way of describing something by comparing it to something else. Look out for the words 'like' and 'as'.

The sails turned slowly like the hands on a clock.

The air was as still as a cat waiting to pounce.

METAPHORS

A metaphor describes something by saying it is something else.

The coffee was molten rock.

This doesn't mean the coffee was actually molten rock, just that it was very hot.

William Shakespeare often used metaphors:

Juliet is the sun.   All the world's a stage.

PERSONIFICATION

Personification means describing things as if they are human.

Once more, the hammer attacked.

The nail looked on, mocking me.

Tip Similes, metaphors and personification are also used in stories. If you're reading a story at the moment, see if you can find any examples.

KENNINGS

A kenning is a poetic phrase which is used to describe something without saying what it is. Here are some kennings for a frisbee:

Cloud skimmer, catch giver, window breaker

QUICK QUIZ

Decide if these are similes, metaphors, personification or none of these.
1 The alarm clock told me to get up.   2 The clouds were marshmallows.
3 A wren is a small bird.   4 He's as cool as a cucumber.

Sound effects in poetry

Poets often choose words for the way they sound. 'Onomatopoeia', 'alliteration' and 'assonance' are sound patterns you might come across.

ONOMATOPOEIA

An onomatopoeia is a word that sounds like the thing it is describing. Here are some examples:

zap

bang, beep, boom, buzz, cock-a-doodle-doo, crack, crunch, fizz, hiss, honk, hum, plonk, plop, pop, roar, rustle, slap, splat, tinkle, zoom

splash

ALLITERATION

Alliteration means using words that have the same initial sound.

Always digging, dark and deep.

Alliteration is often used in tongue twisters like this:

Peter Piper picked a peck of pickled peppers.

Cartoon names like Donald Duck and Mickey Mouse also use alliteration.

ASSONANCE

Assonance means repeating the same vowel sound.

Go brave boat, soaked in foam.

Fair daffodils we weep to see
You haste away so soon. (William Wordsworth)

Tip
Pop music is basically poetry set to music. Listen out for features such as similes, metaphors, alliteration and assonance.

QUICK QUIZ

1 What onomatopoeia is being described? A small bell ringing
2 Use alliteration to make cartoon names for these animals.
   a horse   **b** worm   **c** crocodile
3 Three of these words show assonance. Which is the odd one out?
   girl, world, stone, turn

Story writing – planning

Sometimes, you'll need to come up with your own idea for a story. Other times, you might be given the title, opening sentence or subject for the story. Even if you are given a starting point, you'll still need some ideas of your own.

Have a look around you for inspiration: Is there an article in a newspaper or magazine that could be turned into a great story? Have you seen a spooky house that would make the perfect setting for a mystery?

PLANNING YOUR STORY

Once you've thought of an idea, it's tempting to dive straight in and write your story, but STOP! You must plan your story first. If you can't answer the questions below, you're not ready to start writing.

Plan-tastic!

❶ Who are the main characters?
❷ When and where does your story take place?
❸ How will you begin your story?
❹ What happens in the middle of your story?
❺ How will your story end?

Here's a plan for a story about a boy who finds a gold coin:

❶ Main characters:
Ben – 11-year-old boy, daydreamer, clever ◄── Include brief details about your characters.
Amy – Ben's older sister, bossy, selfish

❷ Setting: Cornwall during summer holiday
Beach – hot, busy, lots of people surfing ◄── Add descriptions you might use in your story.
Museum – modern, large exhibition of coins

The notes in your story plan don't need to be in proper sentences.

❸ Beginning: Ben borrows Amy's metal detector, finds gold coin on beach

❹ Middle: Coin turns out to be rare. Should he sell it? Should he share the proceeds with Amy, as he was using her metal detector?

❺ End: Ben decides to give coin to museum

It's important to know how your story will end before you start writing. Don't just hope you'll think of a good ending when you get there.

Story writing – getting started

THE BEGINNING

Something out of the ordinary should happen at the start of your story. This should send your main character off on an adventure or give him/her a problem to solve.

It's really important to grab the reader's attention straight away. One way to do this is to start with a dramatic event.

Jeff pressed the button for the basement. The lift didn't move, but Jeff started to feel very strange. He went to press the button again, but discovered he couldn't reach. He was shrinking!

Another way to get your readers interested is to start with some dialogue.

"Cheese," said Mike.
"Yikes. There's a bear behind you," shrieked Mildred.
"I'm not falling for that old one!" laughed Mike.
Mildred dropped the camera and ran.

A good beginning will make your readers want to find out what happens next. So it's well worth spending a bit of time getting it right.

SETTING THE SCENE

The setting is when and where the story takes place. When describing your setting, you should use words that suit the mood of your story. For example, you'd use different words to describe a castle in a ghost story to those you'd use in a happy fairy tale.

cold   creepy

dark   spooky

shadowy

warm   charming

magical   beautiful

enchanting

Details about the weather, sounds and smells can all help set the scene.

Be as specific as you can. For instance, don't just say there was a noise – describe it. Was it a crash, a bang or a hiss? How loud was it? See page 26 for more examples of sound words (onomatopoeia).

beep

Story writing – viewpoint

FIRST & THIRD PERSON

There are two viewpoints you can write a story from:

1. You can write as if you <u>are</u> the main character

You are the main character, so write about yourself using '<u>I</u>' and '<u>me</u>'.

> <u>I</u> had been marooned for three months when the idea struck. How could <u>I</u> have been so stupid? The solution had been staring <u>me</u> in the face all the time. <u>I</u> should have used <u>my</u> ...

This is called writing in the '<u>first person</u>'.

2. Or you can write as if you're <u>watching</u> the events

Use '<u>he</u>' or '<u>she</u>' to write about the main character.

> <u>Alex</u> had been marooned for three months when the idea struck. How could <u>he</u> have been so stupid? The solution had been staring <u>him</u> in the face all the time. <u>He</u> should have used <u>his</u> ...

This is called writing in the '<u>third person</u>'.

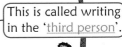

DON'T SWITCH BETWEEN FIRST & THIRD PERSON

Sometimes you'll be given the start of a story and asked to carry it on. If the bit you're given is written in the third person, DO NOT switch to writing in the first person. Look at this example:

> When <u>Mai</u> answered the door, there was nobody there. Looking down, <u>she</u> saw a large cardboard box.

> *<u>I</u> bent down to pick it up, and was surprised how light it was. <u>I</u> shook it gently, but it made no sound. There was no address on it. Was it meant for <u>me</u>?* ✗

The story is about Mai. You're not in it, so don't use 'I' or 'me'.

> *<u>Mai</u> bent down to pick it up, and was surprised how light it was. <u>She</u> shook it gently, but it made no sound. There was no address on it. Was it meant for <u>her</u>?* ✔

Use 'Mai', 'she' and 'her' instead.

QUICK QUIZ

Re-write this passage as if you are Heather (in the first person).

Heather rushed downstairs in her pyjamas. It was her birthday! She couldn't wait to see if there was a shiny, new bicycle waiting for her.

Story writing – characters

PLANNING YOUR CHARACTERS

The people in your story are called characters.

> Characters don't have to be human – they could be talking animals or robots!

All your main characters should appear in your story plan with a few details about them. Make notes about each character's personality, not just what he or she looks like.

CHOOSING NAMES FOR YOUR CHARACTERS

A well-chosen name can give your readers an idea what a character is like. For example, shortened names like 'Billy' or 'Jen' sound informal and friendly.

> Evil is my middle name.

Descriptive names work well for villains, such as Cruella de Vil (cruel devil) in *The Hundred and One Dalmations* by Dodie Smith, or Mr Sowerberry (sour berry) in *Oliver Twist* by Charles Dickens.

DESCRIBING YOUR CHARACTERS

Long, detailed descriptions of a character's appearance can be boring. Choose one or two key features that you want your readers to remember. Try to use descriptions that hint at the character's personality.

Angelica had a long, slender neck. ← This suggests Angelica is elegant.

You can also show someone's personality or feelings by the way they act.

Daisy bounced into the room. ← This suggests Daisy is a lively person (not a ball!).

Pierce hastily snatched the pot and tossed some money at the old woman's feet. ← Pierce seems impatient and ill-mannered.

> **Don't forget** You can also use speech to show your readers what a character is like (see page 31).

QUICK QUIZ

Which of these would be a good name for a strict teacher who is wearing a green jumper?

Mrs Teacher

Mrs Green

Mrs Stern

Story writing – dialogue

Your story will be more interesting if your characters speak. Always try to read your dialogue aloud. Does it sound like a real person speaking?

SHOWING WHAT A CHARACTER IS LIKE

You can use speech to show what your characters are like. For example, you could show that a character is selfish by giving him or her something selfish to say:

"I don't care if you're hungry," said George. "This is my popcorn and I'm not sharing it." ← This shows George is selfish.

You could have just written 'George was a selfish person', but the dialogue is more interesting.

Don't forget You must put speech marks around the actual words that are spoken. See page 11.

HOW DOES THE CHARACTER SAY IT?

Most of the time it's fine to use 'said' to show who spoke. However, sometimes you'll want to make it clear how the words were spoken.

Words you could use instead of 'said'
asked, begged, called, complained, cried, demanded, laughed, moaned, mumbled, pleaded, replied, screamed, shouted, shrieked, sighed, sobbed, suggested, whispered

You can also use an adverb to show how something was said. For example, 'he said nervously' or 'she replied coldly'. (Can't remember what adverbs are? See page 7.)

USING SPEECH TO TELL THE STORY

You can also use speech to tell your readers what's happening in your story, or to give information.

"Quick, he's closing on us," shouted Larry, looking back, "I didn't know bears could run that fast."
"He's after your ice cream, you fool," Luis replied angrily. "Let him have it!"

QUICK QUIZ

"You look cold," said Rachel, "Take my coat."
What kind of person do you think Rachel is?

Story writing – the middle & end

THE MIDDLE – KEEPING YOUR READERS HOOKED

Don't make it too easy for a character to solve his or her problems. Putting one or two extra obstacles in the character's way will keep your readers hooked.

> The water level no longer seemed to be rising, but now Kirk could feel his feet getting wet. His barrel had sprung a leak!

Put your characters in situations where they have to make decisions. This will make your readers wonder what the characters will do next.

> "Let's take the shortcut through the woods," said Meena.
> "We're not allowed," replied her brother, Ali.
> "Well, I'm going that way. You can do what you like." | Ali must decide what to do.

Asking questions is another way to hook your readers – they'll want to know the answers.

> The code Kyle had found made no sense. Could it be someone's initials and phone number? Or a meeting place and date?

LON 190 711

THE END

At the end of your story you must make sure all the problems and mysteries have been solved. Otherwise, your readers will feel let down.

 Don't forget Plan the end of your story before you start to write. If you don't, your story is in danger of fizzling out.

Could your characters overcome their obstacles in a surprising way?

> "It was my metal detector, so I should get half the money," screamed Amy.
> "I agree. We should get the same amount. Nothing," replied Ben. "I've given the coin to the museum!"

Don't forget Once you've finished writing your story you should read it through for mistakes (see page 43).

Plays

WRITING A PLAYSCRIPT

You plan a play in the same way as you plan a story. The only difference is in the way it's laid out. In a playscript, the story is told through the actions and dialogue of the characters.

Set out the playscript with the name of the person speaking on the left, and their speech on the right. Put instructions about how the dialogue should be spoken or what the actors should be doing in brackets. Don't include too many instructions – most of the script should be dialogue.

> Put a colon after the character's name.

> State the setting at the start of the scene.

> Instructions go in brackets.

Scene 1 *In the woods*

(Three friends walk on and stop centre stage)

AMIR: Admit it, Tom. We're lost.

> This is what Amir says. Don't write 'said' or 'asked' in a playscript.

TOM: *(Angrily)* Shut up. We are not lost. I know exactly where we are.

AMIR: Yeah, lost. In the woods. Cold and miles from anywhere.

> Use the dialogue to give more details about the setting.

ISABEL: Stop squabbling you guys. Actually, I can't help thinking we've been through here before.

AMIR: You're right! This is where I snagged my jumper. *(Pulls wool off a branch)* We've been going round in circles. *(To TOM)* Are you still telling me we're not lost?

> Point out any props that are needed.

TOM: *(Looking sheepish)* There must be something wrong with my compass.

ISABEL: Ssshh, listen! I think I can hear voices.

> Plays are a great excuse for dressing up.

Tip As you write a playscript, imagine it being performed. Is it clear what the actors need to do? Will the audience understand what's going on?

QUICK QUIZ

Re-write the following text as a playscript.
"I'm starving," said Amir. "I haven't eaten since lunch."
Isabel took a biscuit out of her pocket and offered it to Amir.

Recounts

A recount is a piece of writing about something that happened in the past. It could be something that happened to you recently, or a true story from history. A recount of someone's life is called a biography (or an autobiography if it's the author's own life story).

PLANNING A RECOUNT

In a recount, you should write about things in the order they happened. Drawing a flow chart will help you get the events in the right order. Here's a flow chart for a recount of a day trip to France:

 6 am got up early ▸ 10 am caught ferry ▸ 1 pm shopped at market ▸ 2 pm visited lighthouse ▸ 4 pm went to vineyard ▸ midnight got back really late

Only include interesting events – miss out boring bits like how long you spent cleaning your teeth.

HOW TO WRITE A RECOUNT

Your first paragraph should set the scene and make it clear what your recount is about.

I had been looking forward to our day trip to France for weeks, but when my alarm clock went off ...

Don't forget The events are in the past, so use the past tense.

Start a new paragraph for each new event on your flow chart.

By the time we arrived at the market, it was very hot. There were a lot of people and the noise was deafening. Most of the stalls were selling ...

◂ Don't just say what happened – add descriptions too.

Use phrases that show the time has moved on. ▸ Later in the afternoon, we visited an old vineyard just outside Calais. There, they were making wine the traditional way, by treading barefoot on the grapes!

Your final paragraph should comment on the events in your recount.

Although it had been a really tiring day, I had enjoyed every minute. ...

QUICK QUIZ

Where would these events go on the flow chart above?

1 almost missed ferry coming back   2 arrived in France

Reports

A report presents facts and descriptions about a particular topic in an organised way. You may be asked to write a report on a topic from history, geography or science.

PLANNING A REPORT

Before you write your report, you'll need to do some research. You could visit the library or look on the internet.

A spider diagram is a great way to organise the information you collect. Here's a spider diagram for a report on sharks:

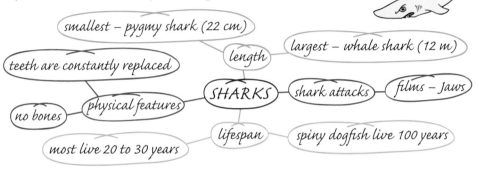

HOW TO WRITE A REPORT

The first paragraph in your report should introduce the topic.

> Sharks are a type of fish. They come in all shapes and sizes, and have been around since before the dinosaurs. ...

Start a new paragraph for each feature on your spider diagram.

> Although sharks have a fearsome reputation, shark attacks on humans are rare. A swimmer is far more likely to drown than be attacked by a shark. ...

They don't scare me.

The final paragraph should summarise your report.

> It is clear that sharks are amazing creatures. ...

QUICK QUIZ

Which bubble on the spider diagram above would you join these to?

1 11 m basking shark washed up in Brighton in 1806

2 only a few sharks are dangerous to humans

Writing letters

Letters can be formal or informal. You send formal letters to people you do not know well or organisations. An informal letter is the sort you would send to a friend or relative.

HOW TO WRITE A FORMAL LETTER

Formal letters should be set out like this:

The address of the person you are writing to goes here.

25 Church Road
Hinkton
HK9 2RU

Put your address in the top right-hand corner.

21st April 2009

Remember to put the date.

Mrs G Anderson
Head Librarian
Hinkton Library
12 High Street
Hinkton
HK9 3ST

Use the person's title (Mr, Mrs, Miss, Dr, etc.) and surname. If you don't know the name put 'Dear Sir/Madam'.

Dear Mrs Anderson,

I am writing to request that you make printed music available at Hinkton Library.

Your first paragraph should explain why you are writing.

Currently I am learning to play the clarinet and need plenty of practice. Although printed music is available at the main library in Midham, it is a long way for me to travel.

Start a new paragraph for each new point.

Furthermore, as Hinkton has its own youth orchestra, I feel sure that printed music would be a very popular addition to the library.

Finish by saying what you would like to happen next. 'I look forward to hearing from you' is a polite way of saying 'write back to me'.

I look forward to hearing from you.

Yours sincerely

Amy Gibson

Miss Amy Gibson

Sign the letter and write your full name underneath.

If you started the letter 'Dear Sir/Madam' change this to 'Yours faithfully'.

 Your letters will sound more formal if you replace everyday expressions like 'I got' with more formal versions like 'I received'.

In a formal letter:
● Don't use contractions like I'm or it's (use I am or it is instead).
● Don't use exclamation marks.

Writing letters

When you're writing an informal letter, imagine you're talking to the person and use the same chatty style.

> You can use everyday language but you must still write in proper sentences.

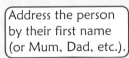

25 Church Road
Hinkton
HK9 2RU

15th May 2009

> Address the person by their first name (or Mum, Dad, etc.).

> You still need your address and the date.

Dear Emma,

How are you? Are you still enjoying university? I'm really looking forward to visiting you next month. Mum's going to bake you a cake!

> Asking questions makes it more like a conversation.

I got picked for the school football team and scored a goal in my first match! Mr Smith said that with a bit of practice I could be the best player in the team. Some of the boys didn't like it when he said that!

> You should still write in paragraphs.

> Contractions such as didn't make it sound informal (see page 14).

A group of us are going to the cinema next week for Katy's birthday. Her dad's taking us all for a pizza afterwards.

> You can use exclamation marks in an informal letter.

See you soon!

Lots of love, Amy xxx

> Finish with an informal phrase, such as 'best wishes' or 'love from'.

> Sign the letter with your first name or nickname.

QUICK QUIZ

Pair up these opening and closing phrases from three letters.

Dear Ben   Yours sincerely

Dear Mr Evans   Yours faithfully

Dear Sir/Madam   With love

Discussions

A discussion gives the arguments for and against a particular issue. You must present both sides of the argument, not just your opinion.

PLANNING A DISCUSSION

When planning a discussion, make a table of arguments for and against the issue. Here are some arguments for and against the building of a new wind farm near Hinkton:

ARGUMENTS FOR	ARGUMENTS AGAINST
● Clean power source ● Fossil fuels will run out, wind won't ● Fossil fuel and nuclear power stations need large amounts of water for cooling. Wind farms do not.	● Spoil the landscape ● Noisy ● 'Shadow flicker' caused by rotating blades ● Birds and bats get injured or killed in the blades

HOW TO WRITE A DISCUSSION

Start by choosing a title that makes it clear what your discussion is about. Then briefly explain both sides of the argument in your introduction.

Should a wind farm be built near Hinkton?
The Hinkton Energy Company would like to build a wind farm near Hinkton. Some residents are enthusiastic, as wind is a good source of clean energy. Others think it will be a blot on the landscape. ...

The rest of your discussion should present both sides of the argument in detail. Where possible, use statements that balance the opposing views.

Although it is often said that wind farms are noisy, studies have shown that modern large turbines make little noise at ground level. ...

Don't forget You're presenting the arguments, not giving your own opinion, so use phrases like 'It is often said that ...' rather than 'I think ...'.

Your final paragraph should be a summary of the different points of view. This is the only place where you could give your opinion. Alternatively, leave it to your readers to make up their own minds.

QUICK QUIZ

Think of two arguments for and two against school uniforms.

Leaflets

A leaflet is usually a small piece of paper, printed on one or both sides. Leaflets are often used to persuade people to buy something, go to an event or to take an action, such as recycling more.

USE LESS PAPER
PICK UP A LEAFLET TODAY!

DESIGNING A LEAFLET

Use plain and simple language when you're writing for a leaflet.

Hinkton Library

The best things in life are free!

Come and see us today at Hinkton Library. You'll receive a warm welcome and find loads to do, even if you're not a member.

What's on offer?

Anyone can use the library to:
- Read newspapers and magazines
- Get free internet access
- Do homework in peace and quiet
- Fax or photocopy documents

It's free to join

Members can borrow books, audio books, CDs, DVDs and games. To make life easier, all these can be reserved or renewed online.

Visit Hinkton Library today!

Open 9am to 5pm, Monday to Saturday
Hinkton Library, 12 High Street, Hinkton

Give your leaflet a main heading that makes it clear what the leaflet is about.

Leaflets often have bright and engaging pictures or use eye-catching colours.

You could include a slogan (catchy phrase).

Write an introduction that tells people what you want them to do.

Using bullet points makes these features stand out.

Use subheadings to break up the text.

Finish with a simple conclusion or call to action.

Include opening hours and contact details if needed.

QUICK QUIZ

Write a slogan for an environmental leaflet persuading people to use less water. Can you think of one that uses alliteration? (Alliteration means using words that have the same initial sound – see page 26.)

Instructions

Instructions tell you how to make or do something, for example, how to make a cake or play a game.

HOW TO WRITE INSTRUCTIONS

When you're writing instructions, write each step as a short command. For example, write 'Turn right at the traffic lights' rather than 'You need to turn right when you get to the traffic lights'.

Don't forget Your instructions should be a series of commands. Don't recount what you did. We grated the cheese. ✗ Grate the cheese. ✔

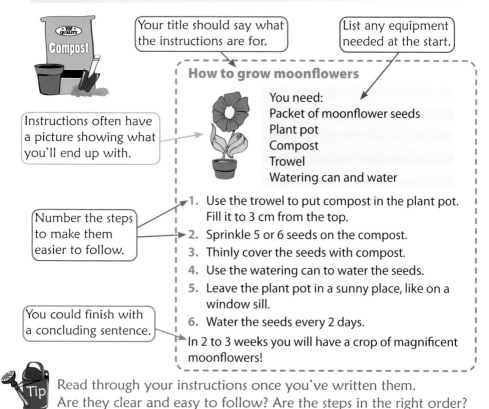

Your title should say what the instructions are for.

List any equipment needed at the start.

Instructions often have a picture showing what you'll end up with.

How to grow moonflowers

You need:
Packet of moonflower seeds
Plant pot
Compost
Trowel
Watering can and water

Number the steps to make them easier to follow.

1. Use the trowel to put compost in the plant pot. Fill it to 3 cm from the top.
2. Sprinkle 5 or 6 seeds on the compost.
3. Thinly cover the seeds with compost.
4. Use the watering can to water the seeds.
5. Leave the plant pot in a sunny place, like on a window sill.
6. Water the seeds every 2 days.

You could finish with a concluding sentence.

In 2 to 3 weeks you will have a crop of magnificent moonflowers!

Tip Read through your instructions once you've written them. Are they clear and easy to follow? Are the steps in the right order?

QUICK QUIZ

Imagine you are making a jam sandwich.

1 What equipment and ingredients do you need?
2 Write down the steps you must follow to make a jam sandwich.

Newspaper reports

HOW TO WRITE A NEWSPAPER REPORT

Newspaper reports are factual, but they must be written in an interesting way. Snappy headlines and eye-catching pictures help grab the reader's attention.

Your headline should catch the reader's interest. Try using a play on words.

Your first paragraph should outline what the newspaper report is about.

Rain sinks festival

Emma Williams Arts Correspondent

Heavy rain on Saturday caused chaos at the first ever Hinkton Music Festival. The campsite was submerged under a foot of water, forcing the event to be abandoned.

Many festival-goers blamed organisers for situating the campsite in the lowest part of the festival site.

"We had a month's rain in one afternoon," responded Mike Brown, a representative of the organising committee. "We couldn't have planned for that."

Despite the crowd's disappointment, spirits remained undampened.

"My tent was washed away, but at least I saved my wellies!" said

Flooding at the Hinkton Music Festival

Anna Symanski, a student at Hinkton College.

Hinkton Fire Brigade were on hand to help evacuate the site, but reported no casualties.

The future of the festival is now in doubt as Hinkton Council have refused to comment on whether a licence will be granted for next year's event.

Include quotations from people involved. Give details about the person you are quoting, such as age or job title.

Your final paragraph should sum up events or comment on what will happen next.

QUICK QUIZ

What's wrong with this newspaper headline? Write an improved version.

Hard-up Hinkton Railways finally decides to close the only train station in Hinkton due to a fall in passenger numbers

Four ways to improve your writing

1. MAKE A PLAN

Whatever type of writing you're doing, you should always make a plan. You'll probably have loads of ideas at the start, but if you don't write them down in a plan, you'll forget what you were going to write next.

 Make sure you know how your piece of writing will end before you start writing it.

2. VARY THE LENGTH OF YOUR SENTENCES

Varying the length of your sentences will make your writing more interesting to read.

As Captain Ford walked back to the rocket, he noticed a large, yellow rock on the other side of the crater. It moved.

Short sentences are great for creating impact. Don't use too many or they'll lose their effect.

 Group related sentences in the same paragraph. This shows that you've organised your ideas. (See pages 12 and 13.)

3. DON'T START ALL YOUR SENTENCES THE SAME WAY

It sounds rubbish if you start all your sentences with the same words.

They went through the gate and up the path. They went up to the door and rang the bell. They went round the back when there was no answer. ✘

Try to start each sentence a different way, like this:

They went through the gate and up the path. When they got to the door they rang the bell. No one answered, so they went round the back. ✔

4. AVOID CLICHÉS

Similes and metaphors are great ways to describe things (see page 25). However, some descriptions like 'as white as a sheet' have been used loads of times before and have become boring. These over-familiar phrases are called clichés and should be avoided like the plague*.

Try to think of your own similes and metaphors.

* Note: 'avoided like the plague' is itself a cliché, and should be avoided like, erm, a pickled wasp sandwich.

Proofreading your work

Once you've finished your work, read it to see if there are any mistakes or things that could be improved. Here are some things to look out for:

CHECK FOR SPELLING MISTAKES

Scan through your work for spelling mistakes. (See pages 15 to 20 for help with spelling.) Although there are no marks for spelling in the writing tests, bad spelling can make it difficult for the reader to understand what you've written.

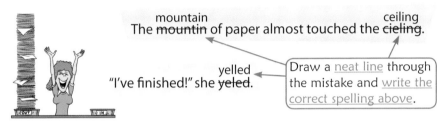

mountain
The ~~mountin~~ of paper almost touched the ~~cieling~~. ceiling

yelled
"I've finished!" she ~~yeled~~.

Draw a neat line through the mistake and write the correct spelling above.

CHECK FOR MISSING OR WRONG PUNCTUATION

Have you missed out any commas or full stops? Do all your questions end with question marks? If you've used apostrophes, check they're in the right place. (See pages 10 to 14 for more on punctuation.)

 Don't join sentences together with commas.

Female kangaroos carry their young in pouches, a baby kangaroo is called a joey.

Female kangaroos carry their young in pouches. A baby kangaroo is called a joey.

DOES WHAT YOU'VE WRITTEN MAKE SENSE?

Imagine how your work would sound to somebody else. If you've written a story, is it clear what's going on? Have you described things as you imagined them? If you've written some instructions, would you be able to follow them?

QUICK QUIZ

There are six mistakes in this passage. Can you find them?

Sarah looked at her her watch nervesly. She was next. Although sh'ed been practising for weaks, she was absolutely petrified. What if she forgot her words. Or tripped as she warked on stage?

Handwriting

Always write as <u>neatly as you can</u>. It's tempting to <u>scribble</u> when you're just writing notes for yourself, but don't or you'll develop <u>bad habits</u>.

SIMILAR LETTERS SHOULD BE THE SAME HEIGHT

- All <u>short letters</u> should <u>sit on the line</u> and be the <u>same height</u>.

  ace cows ← Pay special attention to the letter *s*. It should be the same height as the other short letters.

- <u>Tall letters</u> should be no more than <u>twice the height</u> of <u>short letters</u>.

  m o e s w b d h k l ← Make sure your tall letters are all the same height.

- <u>Capital letters</u> should be roughly the <u>same height</u> as your <u>tall letters</u>.

  Tallest ← Notice that the letter *t* should be taller than the *s* but shorter than the *l*.

- The <u>tails of letters</u> should be roughly the <u>same length</u>. Don't make the tails too long or they'll get in the way when you write your next line.

  o e s w g p q y ← Don't make the tails too fancy – keep them simple.

LETTERS & WORDS SHOULD BE EVENLY SPACED

The <u>letters in a word</u> should be <u>evenly spaced</u>. Don't squash your letters together, but don't leave big gaps either.

<u>Spaces between words</u> should all be the <u>same width</u>.

Letmsleepingmdogsmlie ← Leave roughly enough space to write a letter m between words. (Don't actually write the m!)

DON'T SLANT YOUR LETTERS IN DIFFERENT DIRECTIONS

It doesn't matter whether your letters lean slightly or are upright – just make sure all your letters <u>go the same way</u>.

brilliant ✔ *brilliant* ✔ *brilliant* ✔ *brilliant* ✘

These look neat because in each example the letters go the same way.

This looks messy because the letters slant in different directions.

Crossword

Use the clues below to help you complete this crossword.

Across

1 What does this kenning describe? Time teller (5 letters)
4 What word sounds like 'site', but uses your eyes? (5 letters)
7 Which is the correct spelling: neighbour or nieghbour? (9 letters)
8 Another word for writer (6 letters)
10 'Doing' or 'being' words (5 letters)
13 What is the plural of watch? (7 letters)
14 A paragraph is a group of related _____ (9 letters)
15 Which is the correct spelling: liqiud or liquid? (6 letters)
16 What is the plural of fairy? (7 letters)

Down

1 These can be used to separate the words in a list (6 letters)
2 What is the plural of knife? (6 letters)
3 Names of people, places, animals and things (5 letters)
5 How many syllables are there in the word banana? (5 letters)
6 What type of letter should a sentence start with? (7 letters)
9 A word that means 'full of hope' (7 letters)
11 A colour that rhymes with 'you' (4 letters)
12 The opposite of more (4 letters)
13 What word sounds like 'waist', but is rubbish? (5 letters)

Answers

GRAMMAR, PUNCTUATION & SPELLING

Page 2 Nouns
1 a crowd, stadium, Manchester
  b Judy, dream, horse
2 Manchester, Judy

Page 3 Pronouns
Emma has a pet crocodile. <u>Her</u> brother is scared of <u>it</u> so <u>he</u> won't go in <u>her</u> bedroom.

Page 4 Adjectives
1 a tall, stripy b cold, wet
2 For example:
  a The <u>brave</u> captain remained on the <u>sinking</u> ship.
  b The <u>frightened</u> children crept up the <u>creaking</u> stairs.

Page 5 Comparatives & superlatives
1 younger 2 older 3 youngest

Page 6 Verbs
1 a scored b cycles
2 a They owned a farm. (OR They used to own a farm.)
  b I was feeling cold. (OR I felt cold.)

Page 7 Adverbs
1 sweetly 2 quickly

Page 9 Sentences & clauses
1 but 2 until 3 after

Page 10 Sentence punctuation
The noise started suddenly. What a racket! Where was it coming from? Kate checked the kitchen, the bathroom, the lounge and under her bed.

Page 11 Speech marks
1 "I'll do it later," said Yola.
2 Jen asked, "Why now?"
3 No speech marks are necessary, as this is reported speech.
4 "Attack!" cried the centurion.

Page 14 Apostrophes
1 a Tina can't swim.
  b It's a boy!
  c She'll be here later.
2 a Mark's watch had stopped.
  b The ladies' bags were lost.

Page 15 Spelling by breaking up words
1 a 2 syllables (tad - pole)
  b 3 syllables (diff - i - cult)
  c 4 syllables (in - tro - duc - tion)
  d 3 syllables (um - brel - la)
2 cornflakes, eyeball, bookcase (or casebook)

Page 16 Spelling rules
a quick b curve c badge d believe

Page 17 Homophones
a "I'm <u>bored</u>," yawned Jack.
b I walked on the beach with <u>bare</u> feet.
c Ben jumped <u>higher</u> than Sam.
d You need <u>flour</u> to make a cake.

Page 19 Plurals
a hats b foxes c beaches d leaves
e discos f donkeys g berries h women

Page 20 Prefixes & suffixes
malfunction, unbreakable, childish

READING

Page 21 Reading fiction & non-fiction
1 non-fiction
2 fiction
3 non-fiction

Page 25 Imagery in poetry
1 personification
2 metaphor
3 none of these
4 simile

Page 26 Sound effects in poetry
1 tinkle
2 For example:
  a Harry Horse
  b Wonder Worm
  c Crazy Crocodile
3 stone (all the others have an 'er' sound)

Answers

WRITING

Page 29 Story writing – viewpoint
I rushed downstairs in my pyjamas. It was my birthday! I couldn't wait to see if there was a shiny, new bicycle waiting for me.

Page 30 Story writing – characters
Mrs Stern is a good choice, as stern is another word for strict.

Page 31 Story writing – dialogue
Rachel sounds thoughtful and kind.

Page 33 Plays
AMIR: I'm starving. I haven't eaten since lunch.
ISABEL: (Taking biscuit from pocket) Do you want this?

Page 34 Recounts
1 between 4 pm and midnight
2 between 10 am and 1 pm

Page 35 Reports
1 length
2 shark attacks

Page 37 Writing letters
Dear Ben ➡ With love
Dear Mr Evans ➡ Yours sincerely
Dear Sir/Madam ➡ Yours faithfully

Page 38 Discussions
For example:
Arguments for: School uniforms look smart.

They prevent pupils being picked on because of their clothes.
Arguments against: School uniforms can be uncomfortable. They are unfashionable.

Page 39 Leaflets
For example:
Don't be a water waster!

Page 40 Instructions
1 2 slices of bread, butter, jam, knife
2 Step 1: Use the knife to butter one side of each piece of bread.
Step 2: Spread jam on top of the butter on one of the pieces of bread.
Step 3: Put the two pieces of bread together, with the jam and butter in the middle.

Page 41 Newspaper reports
The headline is too long. You should use a shorter version like 'Hinkton Station to close' or 'End of the line for Hinkton Station'. The details should go in the report.

Page 43 Proofreading your work
Sarah looked at her ~~her~~ watch ~~nervesly~~ nervously. She was next. Although ~~sh'ed~~ she'd been practising for ~~weaks~~ weeks, she was absolutely petrified. What if she forgot her words.? Or tripped as she ~~warked~~ walked on stage?

CROSSWORD

Page 45 Crossword

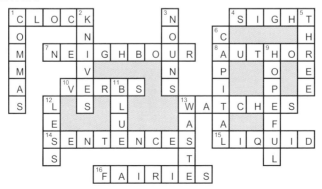

Index